Mercury

by Steven L. Kipp

Content Consultants:
Rod Nerdahl
Program Director, Minneapolis Planetarium

Diane Kane
Space Center Houston

Bridgestone Books
an imprint of Capstone Press

Bridgestone Books are published by Capstone Press
818 North Willow Street, Mankato, Minnesota 56001
http://www.capstone-press.com

Library of Congress Cataloging-in-Publication Data
Kipp, Steven L.
     Mercury/by Steven L. Kipp.
     p.cm.--(The galaxy)
     Summary: Discusses the orbit, surface features, exploration, and
other aspects of the planet Mercury.
     ISBN 1-56065-608-5
     1. Mercury (Planet)--Juvenile literature.   [1. Mercury (Planet)]
I. Title.   II. Series: Kipp, Steven L.   Galaxy.
QB611.K57   1998
523.41--dc21

                                                                97-6918
                                                                CIP
                                                                AC

Photo credits
Charles Harrington, Cornell University Photography, 20
Steven L. Kipp, 6
NASA, cover, 8, 12, 14, 16
New Mexico State University Observatory, 18
Robert Strom, University of Arizona, 10

Table of Contents

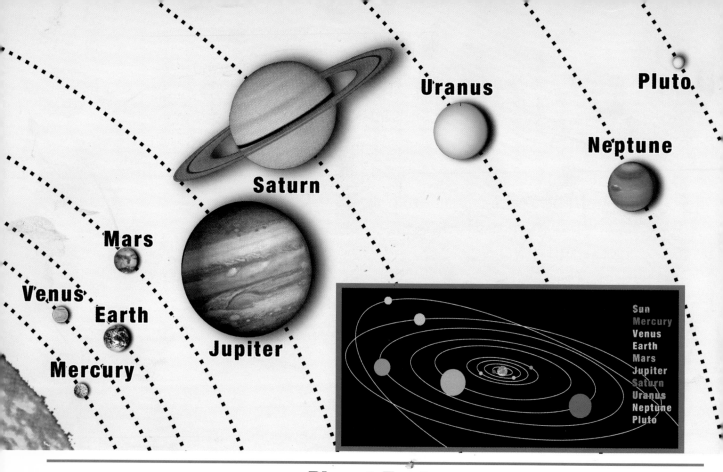

Saturn

Uranus

Pluto

Neptune

Mars

Venus

Earth

Jupiter

Mercury

Sun
Mercury
Venus
Earth
Mars
Jupiter
Saturn
Uranus
Neptune
Pluto

Planet Facts

Mercury

Diameter–3,031 miles (4,878 kilometers)
Distance from Sun–36 million miles (58 million kilometers)
Moons–Zero
Revolution Period–88 days
Rotation Period–59 days

Earth

Diameter–7,927 miles (12,756 kilometers)
Distance from Sun–93 million miles (150 million kilometers)
Moons–One
Revolution Period–365 days
Rotation Period–23 hours and 56 minutes

Mercury and the Solar System

Mercury is part of the solar system. The solar system includes the Sun, planets, and objects traveling with them. The solar system is always moving.

The Sun is the center of the solar system. Everything in the solar system circles around the Sun. The Sun is a star. A star is a ball of very hot gases. Stars like the Sun give off heat and light.

There are nine known planets in the solar system. Planets are the nine heavenly bodies that circle the Sun. Mercury is one of them.

Mercury is the closest planet to the Sun. It is about 36 million miles (58 million kilometers) away from the Sun. Mercury travels at the speed of 107,000 miles (171,200 kilometers) per hour. Mercury rotates as it travels, too. This means it spins.

Scientists have not found living things on Mercury. But they have found some atmosphere. Atmosphere is the mix of gases that surrounds some planets.

Mercury

Planet Mercury

Mercury is the second smallest planet. It is only 3,031 miles (4,850 kilometers) wide. Eighteen planets the size of Mercury could fit into one Earth.

People have a hard time seeing Mercury in the sky. This is because Mercury is close to the Sun. It is always seen near the sun in the sky. The bright light of the Sun makes Mercury hard to see.

People can see Mercury for a few hours about every other month. These hours are around sunrise or sunset. The sky is darker during these times. Then Sun's light does not hide Mercury.

In the past, people thought Mercury was really two planets. This is because it sometimes appears in the eastern sky before sunrise. Other times it appears in the western sky after sunset.

Astronomers learned that Mercury is one planet. Astronomers are people who study stars, planets, and space.

Mercury can be seen for a few hours about every other month.

The Hot and Cold Planet

An atmosphere helps spread heat around a planet. Because Mercury only has a little atmosphere, its temperature changes. Mercury's temperature changes more than 1,000 degrees from day to night.

The side of Mercury that faces the Sun is very hot. The temperature can go up to 800 degrees Fahrenheit (430 degrees Celsius). That is 300 degrees hotter than most ovens can reach.

The side of Mercury that faces away from the Sun becomes very cold. Sometimes the temperature goes as low as -280 degrees Fahrenheit (-170 degrees Celsius). Water freezes at 32 degrees Fahrenheit (0 degrees Celsius).

Liquid water cannot exist on a planet with these temperatures. But scientists think they have found ice on Mercury. The ice is inside holes called craters. Sunlight never shines into these craters. So the ice never melts.

Scientists believe that the craters on Mercury contain ice.

Atmosphere and Magnetic Field

Mercury has almost no atmosphere because of its gravity. Gravity is a force that pulls things down. It keeps things from floating into outer space. Outer space is space outside of a planet's atmosphere. Mercury's gravity is too weak to keep gases around the planet. Instead, the gases float into outer space.

Both Earth and Mercury have magnetic fields. A magnetic field is a force that surrounds magnets. Earth's magnetic field comes from the liquid metal inside the planet. The liquid metal acts like a magnet. The magnetic field helps protect Earth from the Sun's harmful rays.

The inside of Mercury does not have much liquid metal. This means that Mercury's magnetic field is very weak. It does not keep Mercury safe from the Sun.

The inside of Mercury does not have much liquid metal.

Mariner 10

Telescopes helped scientists learn about Mercury. A telescope makes faraway objects look larger and closer. But telescopes had problems. Earth's atmosphere and the Sun's light made it hard to see Mercury. Scientists were not able to see what Mercury's surface looked like.

The Mariner 10 spacecraft helped scientists learn about Mercury's land. A spacecraft is a craft built to travel in outer space. Mariner 10 flew by Mercury in the 1970s.

Mariner 10 sent back television pictures of Mercury's surface. These pictures showed that Mercury is covered by many craters. Meteorites crashed into Mercury and made the craters. Meteorites are large rocks that crash into a moon or planet's surface.

The spacecraft Mariner 10 took pictures of Mercury.

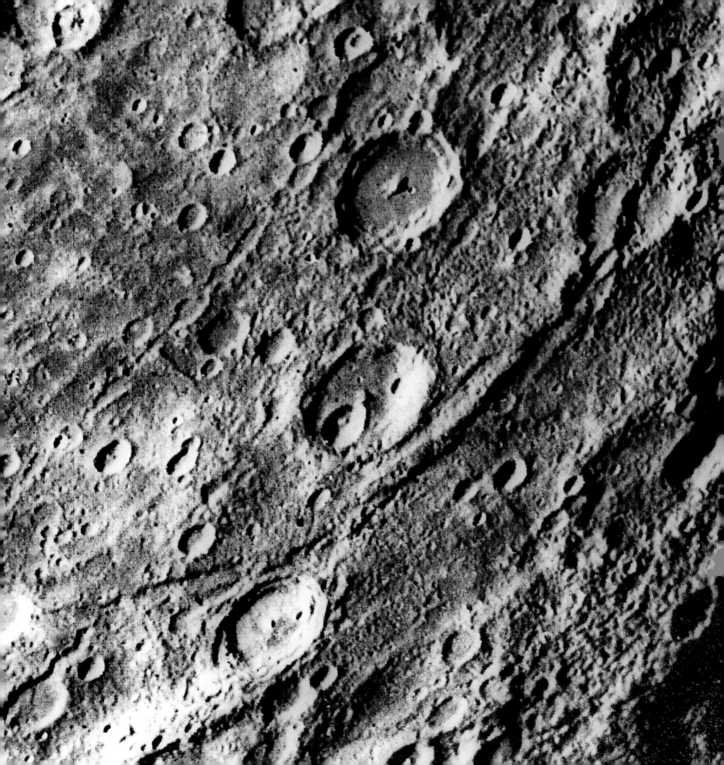

On Mercury

The largest feature on Mercury is the Caloris Basin. A basin is a very large crater. Basins and craters are wide but usually not deep. The Caloris Basin is 800 miles (1,280 kilometers) wide.

A giant meteorite made the Caloris Basin when it crashed into Mercury. The crash was so powerful that rings of mountains formed. These mountains surround the Caloris Basin. The crash formed hills on the other side of Mercury, too.

Mercury also has large splits on its surface. The splits are so large that pieces of land dropped into them. This formed cliffs called scarps. Sometimes scarps stretch for many miles or kilometers across the land.

Flat land lies between Mercury's craters and splits. These smooth areas are called planitia. Liquid rock called lava made the planitia. Lava filled the craters and hardened. Astronomers believe the planitia are thousands of years old.

Cliffs called scarps stretch across Mercury.

Rotation and Revolution

Mercury spins as it moves through space. It takes Mercury 59 Earth days to spin around once. This is called a rotation. Rotation time also makes up a planet's day. Mercury's day is almost as long as three months on Earth.

Mercury circles the Sun like Earth does, too. One complete circle is called a revolution. A planet's revolution time makes up its year. It takes Mercury 88 days to circle the Sun once. This is faster than any other planet. It takes Earth 365 days to circle the Sun.

Early Italian people named the planet after their god Mercury. These Italians believed he was a messenger for all the gods. His winged shoes made him very fast. The people believed that both the god and the planet were fast.

Mercury's day is almost as long as three months on Earth.

Phases and Solar Day

People watching Mercury with a telescope will see that it seems to change shape. But Mercury does not really change shape. The Sun lights different parts of it.

From Earth, people can see only the part of Mercury that the Sun lights. The part that people see is called a phase. Earth's moon shows phases, too.

Mercury's rotation and revolution speed help scientists measure its solar day. The solar day is the time from one noon to the next noon. Mercury's solar day is 176 Earth days long. It is longer than Mercury's year.

Mercury shows phases as the Sun lights different parts of it.

Parts of Mercury

The core is the center part of Mercury. It is more than 2,250 miles (3,600 kilometers) thick. The core is made of liquid rock and metal.

The outer part of Mercury is called its crust. The crust is made of solid rocks. The solid rocks float on the liquid metal of the core. Mercury is one of the four planets that has a rocky surface. Earth has a rocky surface, too.

Scientists have learned many things about Mercury. But there are still questions that need to be answered. Scientists use large telescopes to study Mercury. Someday scientists might send another spacecraft to Mercury. This would help people learn more about both Mercury and the solar system.

Scientists use large telescopes to study Mercury.

Hands On: Make Craters

Mercury is covered with small and large craters. Meteorites formed the craters when they crashed into the planet. You can make your own craters with mud and pebbles.

What You Need

An empty pie plate
Mud
Pebbles and small rocks

What You Do

1. Fill your pie plate with mud.
2. Drop some pebbles and small rocks on the mud.
3. Leave the pebbles and rocks in the mud. Let the mud dry for several hours.
4. Remove the pebbles and rocks. There are now craters in the mud.

Craters on Mercury form like this. The mud is like the land on Mercury. The pebbles and rocks are like the meteorites that crash into Mercury.

Words to Know

astronomer (uh-STRON-uh-mur)—a person who studies stars, planets, and space

basin (BAY-suhn)—a very large crater

crater (KRAY-tur)—a hole in the ground made by a meteorite

phases (FAZ-ess)—the different amounts of a moon or planet lit by the sun

revolution (rev-uh-LOO-shuhn)—one body circling another like planets circle the Sun

rotation (roh-TAY-shuhn)—to spin around

scarp (SKARP)—a cliff formed by cracks in a planet's surface

Read More

Simon, Seymour. *Mercury*. New York: Morrow Junior Books, 1992.

Vogt, Gregory. *Mars and the Inner Planets*. New York: Franklin Watts, 1982.

Useful Addresses

NASA Headquarters
300 E Street SW
Washington, DC 20546

National Air & Space Museum
Smithsonian Institution
Washington, DC 20560

Internet Sites

Kids Web—Astronomy and Space
http://www.npac.syr.edu/textbook/kidsweb/astronomy.html

The NASA Homepage
http://www.nasa.gov/NASA_homepage.html

StarChild: A Learning Center for Young Astronomers
http://heasarc.gsfc.nasa.gov/docs/StarChild/StarChild.html

Index